Motorcycle Meanderings

25 Motorbike Essays
Strictly for the Bathroom

Johnny Winterer

ROAD
BOOKS

ISBN: 0990009017
ISBN-13: 978-0-9900090-1-6

DEDICATION

To my brother Mike. Thank you for putting me on motorcycles my whole youth. You planted one of the most important ideas in my soul, that has sustained me on the deepest level. Eternally grateful.

CONTENTS

Motorcycle Meanderings

MOTO BUM

Today I found myself doing something I always do. I rode my usual route on Pacific Coast Highway 1 to Malibu to meet with a client. Lovely ride along the ocean. Beats riding on Highway 101 along the caged hamsters fighting for asphalt real estate. After meeting my client, when I was heading home, I saw a side road that looked good and twisty. Instead of taking the straight shot back home, I did what I always seem to do. I saw that this deviating mountain road that juts out of the coast would add miles upon miles of twisted, snaking roads on the spine of this unexplored mountain...perfect. Of course I played the cursory 5-second rational mind game to decide if I should do it, then without another thought, I did a U-turn, with a crook in my smile and a glint in my eye.

As I wound my way around the mountain's hips, I realized I am a bum. Knowing how little is in my bank account, I should be racing home to build more business. But I have been this way since childhood. Homework was always something to start at 10 at night because the day was meant for exploring. Then twenty years of ski bumming damaged my work ethic forever. And even though I admire the Protestant work ethic of America, I resonate more with my European and Latin ancestors, who subscribe to a "work to live" philosophy instead of a "live to work" ethos. So this means I have a lazy bone to most but a sane, balanced life to me. So any chance I can, I go play, as long as the food, shelter and gas-in-the-tank needs are met.

Yes, I am a moto bum.

The detour was worth it. The extra fourteen miles gave me time to do my daily reflection and sort out the trash talk in my head. I prioritized what mattered most. Somehow, dreaming and planning to sell a few bikes so I could buy a Ducati got in there with paying the phone bill. Then the idea of writing this little ditty cropped up ahead of looking for a new home, even though I only have five days left in my present shelter. Such a vagabond, such a bum. Did skiing ruin me, or was it motorcycles? What killed my climb-up-the-ladder spirit? Maybe I've always been this way and simply found the right activities to support my lifestyle. All I know is that I will keep taking side roads. I may not get there efficiently, but I will certainly enjoy the gettin'. Right on. Write on. Ride on.

FUCK CARS

A dear friend, who witnessed my metamorphosis from non-biker to moto-nutter, saved a t-shirt from back when he was heavy under the trance of motorbikes. He gave this shirt to me as he knew I had been bitten hard by the bug. This was a gesture of love, recognizing I was a fellow soldier, a comrade in arms, a motorcyclist with passion and zeal. For the black t-shirt has a black and white photo of a WWI soldier on his relic of a motorcycle, holding a machine Tommy gun that is pointed straight at whatever is ahead. The soldier's determined look says it all—I am going to shoot what I am looking at. The title underneath the provocative vintage photo says in plain, large white words, "Fuck Cars."

Yes, fuck the caged beasts that keep us safe from the fresh smell of flowers and the cold air at the bottom of a hill. I believe that riding in cars is passive movie-watching of the outside world. The driver, if sane, should throw a rock through the windshield and bust out the cracked glass, so that he and the passengers can feel the cold of morning on their faces, the smell of flowers in spring, and the heat of Vegas on their eyes. Be in the movie of life, not watching behind shatterproof, clear screens, rolling lifeless on four wheels, yawning. Life is for feeling and being, not watching.

But breaking a car windshield won't do. Because when you ride a motorcycle, you engage your stomach muscles and feet and hands in a way that has a direct impact on the course of trajectory. Curve your right foot, and the bike goes right. Wiggle your butt and the bike swerves, gently rolling. Smiling, for some unknown reason, has a direct link to the throttle, and makes one bear down on the grunting beast. Dare scream for joy in your helmet, and your bike does 80 mph before you can stop hooping.

Cars have insulated us from the world we were designed by the evolutionary god to be part of. That is a sin. To be of this world and not enjoy the wind, the gritty sand in your teeth, the cold snot in your nose—these are crimes against all that is good and moral.

Look at what it takes to move one person to work in a car of 4000 pounds of heaving hard plastic and cheap metal. Most people are moving alone in their car. Just driving in LA shows that only a very small portion (I bet 5%) has an additional passenger. Other parts of the globe are not so attached to their two-ton caged monsters. Go to Rome for instance, and see how many people use motorbikes to move their one person. In Italy most teens don't drive cars. They are expected to have a Vespa scooter or moped for many years. My Northern Italian ex-girlfriend said all the kids in high school ride mopeds. It's a way of life. Teens don't get cars, they get parent-approved scooters, motorbikes, and other two wheeled steel horses. I think motorbikes match the teen spirit much more than a big old cage because teens love freedom. Their spirit has not been squelched by the machine of Hamster Wheel Culture. Lets learn from the European children and get the shackles off.

In Asia, whole families ride together...sign of poverty? Not always. Rather a sign of people that embrace the world outside and adapt. How many times have I seen photos of little Hondas, Suzukis, and Kawasakis hauling cargo of chickens, produce, or bamboo in Thailand, Nepal, Burma for an enterprising young man, supporting his family. Big rigs are not always needed.

In the good ole US of A, people can't wait to get their 300 horsepower $30,000 Ford Mustang to show off and lay down lots of rubber. Or they have the new Volkswagen GTI that can go 0-60 in six seconds...a civilian street ready 3000-pound missile. I am a red blooded American and rarely has a car made me feel what a motorbike has. When I was a teen, the only times that I truly liked my cars, I was doing highly illegal maneuvers that were dangerous. I got more joy out of scrambling down a dirt road on an Indian 100 dirt bike when I was ten-years-old, or a Honda 50 minibike at age seven, never getting out of first gear because I did not know there was more than one gear.

Motorcycles make me nonrealistic, and I like that. In my ideal world, the only people that should be in cars are old people, and even then I would suggest a three-wheeler motorcycle to compensate for balance issues. You're never too old to feel alive.

Well, I know cars are here to stay. But goddamn them if they get in my way. Make room for me and my motorbike, and my invisible Tommy gun. Yes, "Fuck Cars," the necessary evil of our highway culture. Make room for my motorcycle and my fellow riders. We are a people who are called to arms to defend our freedom. We simply don't like cages.

And you, if all you do is drive a car or truck, consider getting out of the comfort of glass-covered cages, and smell the world. Chuck your Iphone, Ipad, Icar and leave the

Cyborg existence of caged safety. Feel the world, freeze your ass off, and become one with your own movie, your own life, one with the green earth, one with the Maker, one with the motorbike. Pretty soon, you'll be wearing the black t-shirt and wondering why you ever bothered with prison bars on wheels.

SUNRISE WITH TRUCKERS

The other day I was leaving Salt Lake in the early morning darkness. It would turn out to be a long 900-mile day of twelve hours seat time, plus a couple more hours for gas, Denny's and Starbucks stops. I left early because I did not want the traffic, and I found solace out on the high desert of Utah's I-15. Speed limit is 80 mph, so I got her up to 85 and just cruised. I watched the sunrise with the Truckers.

I had actually come up from California during the night two weeks before. I was avoiding the LA snail pace, cluster fuck traffic so I left at 9pm in hopes of hitting LA to Vegas in the middle of the night. Again, I traveled all through the night with truckers as my only companions.

I realize the truckers and I have a lot in common, minus the sixteen wheel difference. We even like the same restaurants. We gas up at the same Flying Js and drink Folgers at the Denny's bar together. We share stories about the road. The fewer words spoken, the better. We are both fluent in the same silent language of the night.

We learn to sit for hours with our motors and the forever-straight interstates that tempt us to slumber. But we Red Bull it up and add a little Lynyrd Skynyrd or George Jones, and keep our minds focused on the task of observing nature at its unmolested finest.

We like uncrowded highways. We want them all to our selfish selves. So we wake up early or get on the road late to avoid the snickering hustle and bustle of caged rats and gerbils and hamsters.

We want to witness the mysterious night unfurl into the waking of day. When I'm alone with the dawning silhouette of mountains and sandstone, inhaling the smell of fresh sage and juniper, I find a solace that soothes my soul. The night sky rains shooting stars, a cool pocket of pine trees whisper to me. It's almost like there are two worlds—the world of man and the world of god. The truckers and I, we like the world of god, when man sleeps and god is awake.

And then dawn comes, and with it a profound sadness. To see the roads fill up with hurried beasts who did not see the innocence of the night, who do not know its quiet, wild sublimity.

Truckers are my kin. I hope they get to drop their 18 wheels and saddle a two-wheeler sometime, just because they already get it. That is my prayer.

CHURCH

One day a buddy of mine who is deeply committed to his own recovery from addiction and is very committed to his faith said, "Better to think about God on the motorcycle than be in church thinking about your motorcycle." Amen.

I am a religious soul. I was steeped in Catholic.

Jesus.

I was that guy who became the youngest altar boy and snuck more wine and handfuls of unblessed hosts in my mouth like crackers than my contemporaries. Good gig for a grade-schooler. Then in grad school, I snuck in a credential in pastoral counseling. I even considered the priesthood all the way into my early thirties.

Geezus.

Well, I still have the spirit, and it soars now on two wheels. I don't go to church anymore, and I don't believe any less. I doubt, like any rational ape, and I also believe that little thread of invisible intuition is onto something much larger than me. Addicts have a higher power whether it is mother earth, god, Shiva, their children, or their passion, whether surfing, skiing, golf, or motor biking.

Motorcyclists have their own religion.

If you've ever wondered whether bikers are spiritual, go to a biker rally, and you'll feel a religious fervor that rivals tent revivals. BMW people can ride twelve hours a day for a week or more to an ever-elusive shimmering shrine in the distance.

Beemer folk spend inordinate times convincing their souls that the boxer motor invented by a guy named Fritz, is the best way to experience the flight of riding, because that motor originally was based off an airplane motor. Go to a BMW rally, and you will see five thousand tents of Bedouins who believe in what they do. Words don't need to be spoken, but with some German beer and bikes they are having a cheerful Communion. It is a sublime community that is "committed."

Harley folks are downright scary religious with Lynyrd Skynyrd and leather. They embrace a little of the shadow side of spiritual mythology—they may believe in Jesus, but they believe in the badass Jesus who likes to drink and swear a bit. They like the Jesus who drove the merchants out of the temple. The mad Jesus. They know Jesus would have worn leathers and mixed freely with their kind. They appear to be the direct descendants of the Viking Pagans.

Ducati people are into that Roman hedonistic-naked-orgy-religion that oozes sex and bleeds Ferrari red. Triumph folks are grounded in the Celtic, Guinness-drinking, cigarette-smoking, road-racing pilgrimage we call the Isle of Man TT...just fuckin nuts and I admire them with pure jealous desire. The Japanese bikes? Well those folks have a little Satan in their tank. They invented the real bullet bike. They believe in real speed. Period. You get some of those believers on a Gixxer or YZ something, and get outta their way because their Katana, Hayabusa, Interceptor says it all, "Get outta my way because I'm popping wheelies to the god of sky at 120mph."

Just like all religions, we are trying to touch something divine. So the world has its religions and we bikers or motorcyclists have ours. Don't all faiths speak the same language on some level? Radicals would say, "hell no." But they are the rigid ones who only like their particular brand of religion. They have not learned the humility of knowing that we don't know shit. The numinous, the unknowable, the mystery is what matters in my book.

So many of us neo-pagans think god is out on the highway. We feel connected to life divine while rumbling down the tarmac. We know others look at us and judge. We don't mind. I don't feel one iota of guilt when I ride on Sunday Sabbath. Not once have I thought, "Should I be in church?" Because I am sitting in my pew, genuflecting, hearing the gospel of wind, sun, water, and fire. The fire of combustion. Praise the Lord.

MOTORCYCLE MEANDERINGS

WHAT I HAVE LEARNED

In the years I have entrusted my soul to the motorcycling gods, I have learned a bit. I have learned that I am powerless over my need to ride. It is beyond desire. It's not a love/hate relationship, as many relationships turn out. It is a love/love relationship. The cost is my hard earned money for gas, tires, and oil. That's a fair price for an experience that feeds my soul, a humble tithing to the motorcycle gods.

Who else benefits from this most self-loving activity? All those I come into contact with. I am more in love with the world and life; I have passion and joy to truly share. I have also learned that bikes don't like neglect. They don't need to be pretty, but they do need to be maintained. Ironically, I have applied this lesson to maintain my body and soul as well. I doubt I would have quit my intolerably toxic job if the bike hadn't taught me I could be so much happier. I realized I didn't have to settle for mediocre survival; I could thrive and feel joy beyond words. At mid-life there were still challenges I could spend a lifetime pursuing. I became childlike in spirit again and realized how jaded and cynical I had become. The bike became the light that shone through the darkness of this tough, old world.

The bike got me off the hamster wheel that leads men to early graves. I quit trying to please the sycophantic culture and became my own man again. I became an entrepreneur and respected my god given ability and gifts. I remembered who I truly am...a man of adventure and exploration. Yes, I risk, now more than ever.

I have also learned that I know so little. I barely know how a motor works no matter how much I read about it and tinker. I am humble before the engineers and men of invention for giving me such a fine creature to ride. You brilliant men who are artists, designers, metallurgists, physicists—I am forever in your debt. You have given me something simple and beautiful to appreciate—functional, sensual art in motion.

I learned that love was possible again. I learned that real friends root for you and your true desires, and those that are afraid, well they judge and condemn. I realized the wisdom of being truly self-responsible. When you ride a motorbike, the cost is so high that there is whole new level of responsible living and being truly present. Bikers put their lives in danger if they don't take full responsibility for what they are doing or are not present. I learned I can't fuck around, that life is very real, very short and very precious. My two-wheeled steed taught me not to take any of this for granted.

I would not call this religion as I don't want to desecrate this experience with structure and theology. But riding is nothing short of spiritual. I have reasons and meaning to this stardust experiment we call life. And it beckons me to live long, experiencing as much as I can before my time is up. I want to keep my spirit free, my soul grounded in earth and asphalt, and my mind free of human contrived bullshit. I want to be free, and I know my path. This is my gospel, my truth.

HWY 33

I moved to Ojai, California three years ago, driven by pure serendipity and desperation. Lost my fiancée and hated my employer. I was running from pain and exhaustion, and landed in the motorcycle land of milk and fuckin' honey.

Today, after realizing that being my own boss has made me forget to vacation, I decided to ride. Highway 33, which lies a mile from my home, is motorcycle Nirvana on this heavenly earth. If you think Tail of the Dragon is special, you have to come out and ride the twisties of 33. Expect fifty miles of turns that arc like a mistress's hips.

How is it that the first half of a ride feels like exorcising the demons of the day, and the last half is like blissing out after a massage? I like to decide my endpoint before I ride, usually the top of a mountain pass, where I ride like holy hell and join the dance of my twin 1100cc. I take a piss at the top and sail home like the demon has left my belly and become an angel.

Back to Highway 33. The temptations are too great for mortal man to not want to do a fast dance. As you lean into the curve at 40, you can almost touch blooming lupines. Pull off to see the ocean, a glistening blue gem twenty miles in the distance. The road takes you from elevation 400 to 5200 feet in less than twenty minutes, and the switchbacks remind you of the pioneers who paved their way by horse. Now on your horse, you feel like you are hiking on two wheels, a modern pioneer exalted with the same sense of discovery. You look out over the next turn to a hawk soaring fifty paces away at eye level. Flying while you fly.

Before you die, if you are 200 miles in the vicinity of Los Angeles, you will need to escape the conference, your partner, your kids, your dog, your motor home. Leave the beach, and go find God on Hwy 33. It's an expedition, a holy sermon and an elemental massage, all on one stretch of sacred mountain.

MOTO "GUY"

They say things happen in threes. In less than twelve hours, three separate people said I needed to meet this guy, named Guy. One of the three clarions actually called Guy and found out when he would be giving a tour of his own personal museum. Guy Webster is of Ducati fame. At one time, he owned the largest collection of Ducati's in the world. He also happens to be a world-renowned photographer. Well, as fate would have it my "new" 13-year-old bike had been part of his "old" collection of motorcycles, which I bought through a third party a month before I met Guy. Confusing. Too much synchronicity for this boy to ignore.

This man humbly took a few families and me on a private tour of his collection of mostly Italian bikes. I could tell most of the visitors were neophytes and could barely understand the rarity and interest of each unique bike. After the first hour they were getting restless, while I was just warming up. I don't fault these folks, as they are the sane, balanced ones of the world who have fuller lives outside of bikes. But me, well, I was in rapture and could have listened to Guy talk all day. This man is beyond passionate. He owned six hundred bikes at one time and has restored hundreds more over the last thirty years. He collects the most rare racing pedigrees and key technological advancement bikes that have changed the world.

Guy taught me all about the love of motorcycles. He gave me permission to be who I am. Sometimes, I need that. Even at my middle age, I need to be reminded that it's okay to be fully engaged in one's obsessions and passions. I can't help that motorcycles have me by the short hairs. And my soul is elevated when I meet someone like Guy, who revels in his love without excuse or embarrassment, who embraces his nature and has obviously not limited his success with his "hobby."

I was the last to leave Guy and his museum. I did not want to. I felt like I had made a new friend. He was the grandfather type who you just want to hang out with, hear his stories and gain real wisdom about life. He readily admitted he was obsessed and crazed about his passion. Somehow he managed to remain married and raise a family amidst spending his adult life racing, collecting, restoring. I realized his mind and soul are the museum as much as the bikes resting under his protection. He is the curator and godfather of all moto bikes Italian. As the stickers on all his bikes and my new one say, he is "MotoGuy."

His life echoes the wisdom my dad taught me, "Go for it." So if you are a schmuck like me who has fallen under the siren song of moto spirits, then do it. Go for it.

SOMETHING VISCERAL GRABS

Why do I ride motorcycles? Because something grabs me deep down in my soul. It is sexual. It is primal. It's the part of me that worships the human body and sensuality. I've had this urge with particular models of motorcycles, and everyone has their own taste. I love all bikes and believe riders fall in love with whatever deep down resonates. It's a commitment of sorts. But I do fall in love with all kinds of motobikes and would buy and ride those too if I had a fat wallet.

I love the Ducati Sport Classic Paul Smart edition. I love Dakar race bikes, adventure dual sport, scramblers, cruisers, rat bikes, and even choppers. I lust after any café racer because I am easy. Slut like. Every rider has their tempting, lustful beauty, and with the limits of money and time, we have to choose one or just a few models at a time.

When I first saw my 2003 BMW F650gs Dakar, I knew it was the steed for me. I cannot really put words to it. It was something I loved from the second I saw a picture. I spent hundreds of hours researching everything about it and looking at every picture I could find, every angle. Pornography. Pure and simple. Enough to cause serious jealousy issues with my ex-fiancée.

Once that wild mustang thoroughbred BMW Dakar stood with a red bow in my parking lot at work (delivered from Florida to Durango, Colorado), I knew this bike would be my friend. I quickly called him "Pepe the Mule." My reliable mule taught me the purest joy of life next to love, family and friendship.

This is my first "real" bike to call my own, and I will be forever faithful. How can one ever forget the first one that made the whole world come alive? There is always the first. Just like a high school sweetheart, there can only be one.

How many times have I heard the melancholic grief of someone longing for the first motorcycle they regretted selling? I will never sell Pepe. Ever. I will not long in regret for the beast that tamed my heart and set it afire with soulful wildness and repose. Ironic paradox.

Other bikes have had my heart, and I do not talk to Pepe too much about it. He knows. He tolerated me riding my R100 café racer and Triumph Sprint. Now that I sold them, he puts up with his German cousin, a red R1100S. He understands that because the R1100S is for different journeys and work. Pepe is for the rough dirt roads and slower pace country roads where I can really enjoy the scenery and smells. The red dragon R1100s knows its job is chewing up miles on the coastal Hwy 1 in Big Sur and taking me to MotoGP races at Laguna Seca and World Superbike races at Miller Motorsports in Salt Lake. I am striking a balance with my German bikes, and neither knows which is my mistress and which is my mate. The Kawasaki Ninja was for asphalt track days exclusively and the Suzuki DR 350 was for lightweight ripping sideways on dusty dirt forest roads, rocks spitting, tail wagging.

I may have to get a separate garage bedroom wall, so they don't see me bring home a Ducati or Harley. Better yet, I rent the Harleys so I can taste all of them, and my bikes will never need to know. The future Yamaha, Indian, Husqvarna, Moto

Guzzi, though, well, I am obviously polyamorous. And there is no end to love.

MOTORCYCLE MEANDERINGS

RIDING WITH A RAMBLING MAN

John is playing irreverent gospel tunes in my local Ojai coffee shop, Bohemia. John is a man of great spirit and spent a fair amount of his life drinking spirits. Now that he is in recovery, he seems to have put his energy into motorcycle riding. When I first met him, he would leave me in the dust. What am I saying? He still leaves me in the dust. Something about his head and body placement makes him look like a Moto GP racer just going around a regular canyon turn. You can tell he has spent his life on the edge, as his body seems to lean over another edge with frightening aggression.

Even his music tonight is there on that precipice. He is playing Hank Williams the Third! That ain't no gentle, weepy country. Hank speaks of life on the dark, shadowy side and knows where to place the word "fuck" perfectly in a song. Now John is singing about his past life of women and fire, one of his own songs. Soon he will be singing of Jesus. John is a Christian.

He would not be alive if it weren't for recovery, Jesus, and motorcycles. A loving friend, who knew of his passion for all things two wheels, gave him a brand new Honda VFR to redeem his soul and reclaim his spirit. John grew up with a father who raised him amongst motorcycles, mostly Hondas. He is pure grace to watch. Just as he once put everything on the line when partying, he now does this with his music and motorcycling. John does not know anything less than full throttle. But he is learning.

John and his partner were about to buy my 2000 Triumph Spring RS, a screaming triple 955cc with 110hp, for her. She was so jonesing for that yellow, beautiful, muscular machine, and John knew that bike would be his second steed whenever he wanted...smart man.

The same week she was about to buy my Triumph, she had an intuition not to, and found out she was with child days later. John is singing right now a song about how youth is wasted on the young.

John is about to be a father. Boy, how his riding has changed. He now rides with me and some old guys, who believe in the mantra, "There are bold riders and old riders but very few bold, old riders." John is making the salvation journey, from a bold to (hopefully) an old rider, father and husband. John is getting married in two months.

John rides his motorcycle just as gracefully, and I can now keep up because he has slowed his pace just enough for me to see him disappear into the next foggy turn. I wonder what he dreams of as he rides—his love and future wife? His new life coming into this world? The next bend in the road?

Amen, John. Keep us riding into our dreams.

THE GREAT EQUALIZER

Yesterday I attended a gathering of cult-like believers, who show up every year for Guy Webster's Spring Open House. This famed motorcycle guru is known around the world for his private selection. He is generous with his time and energy, laboring with the ignorant to educate them on the merits of his beautiful historical collection. But this essay is not about Guy Webster, it's about all the nutters who showed up on their two wheels to celebrate their mutual passion. There must have been about 500 bikers. Not only did we get to glory in Guy's collection, but we got to ogle each other's bikes.

I realized that day, that motobikes equalize humanity in a brother and sisterhood, a moto-humanhood. As I stood amongst seven other gents staring at the one bike in the center, like a glowing campfire, I started to dialogue with the fellow next to me for about a minute or two. We had not made eye contact as we fawned with our words about why we were in love with the Moto Guzzi V7. Our conversation felt brotherly, as if he knew my soul and I, his. He said, "We must like this bike because our generation grew up with these types of bikes." The statement resonated, and now I wanted to see the age of the man that spoke.

As I turned to gaze at him, I realized I knew this man. I had seen him in countless movies my whole life. He looked more ragged in real life without the falsity of the camera and makeup. The real human was just a man. I kept my cool. I did not want to stop talking about motorcycles with him, as I am sure most people want to just talk about his Hollywood life. And it was effortless to continue our enjoyable dialogue about the beautiful Guzzi. Because we were two humans who had childhood memories on Enduros and bikes of the Seventies. If I had been at a movie premier, our conversation would have lasted all of five panic attack, hero-worship, nervous seconds until I would have moved on after a quick handshake.

But this encounter was actually calm and pleasing. He may have sensed through my poker face that I recognized him, but we just moved through that 1/10th of a second and kept on about the Guzzi until all that was left was silent appreciation with no more words, just speechless—two brothers in spirit wondering when we would or if we could get our own Guzzi. Our eyes were young again.

As I walked away from that bike, another buddy said, "Isn't that someone famous?" I kept walking away, intent on not disturbing my moment, as my buddy turned and went to do the "meet the actor" thing that most of us would normally do. I just kept walking, ready to meet the next motorbike or nutter.

Later that day, another friend at the event noted that, "We are all the same here. We all have this common bond." It didn't matter who you were standing next to. All hierarchy of our culture disappeared. Imagine a tribe where all spoke the silent language of appreciation and beauty. Sure some in the crowd were wealthy and powerful by other standards. But somehow among all these varied motorcyclists, there was a kindred connection and appreciation for the metal craft, the pinstriped paint, the vision of each rider customizing his craft. I'm talking about something spiritual and highly intangible in our souls. There was an unspoken reverence for each machine and rider. Of the half thousand connoisseurs, there was no tension, no posturing, just brotherly love. Something felt equal in the air.

The motobike was our common link to each other. Maybe that is why I love these machines. I found my tribe, my one place where emotional safety leads to genuineness and true freedom of self. My brothers and sisters know me and I them. We share into our common experience, telling our stories, our primal mythology.

Later that day I heard that that Guzzi V7 was Guy's favorite in his collection. Same with me, the seven gents, and that famous guy, whoever he was.

MOTORCYCLE MEANDERINGS

THE BEST MONEY SPENT

Oh, my butt!! I am a long-suffering fool. I can put up with inordinate amounts of discomfort and have paid the dear price too often. I am the guy that will ride in a snowstorm without heated anything. It is my folly and weakness.

For all its glorious technology, BMW cannot seem to make a "saddle" that feels good. Sure, make a motor that can last forever; I once met a guy who had 850,000 miles on his 1978 R100RS with only two top end rebuilds. Sure, make a bike that loves to go all day and purrs like a sewing machine. But is it that hard to make a seat that fits my ass and feels good? If I am going to ride eight hours, I can only do so if my derriere is comfortable. But no, after two hours, this dull ache becomes a searing tortuous pain all through my spine. This physical pain soon can become mental suffering.

Because I love motorcycling around everywhere and salivate at the idea of a weeklong trip for thousands of miles, I am my own Grand Inquisitor. Who needs medieval torture instruments when we have BMW making seats?

BMWs are expensive, and the technology is cutting edge. Why, oh why would they skimp on the seat? Are they trying to keep the cottage industry of custom saddle makers in business? Are these saddle makers slipping BMW some cash behind closed doors, whispering, "Hey, keep making shitty saddles. Find the cheapest most painful materials and put spikes and burrs under the vinyl fake leather."

Anyone who loves to travel long distance typically has a custom saddle. They start around $300 for the Sergeant or Mustang saddles and can cost closer to $400 or $500 for a custom job. Only after you have experienced the crucifying agony of a very sore arse can you understand the rationalizations and justifications of spending a fortune on a form-fitted foam seat that is literally carved to fit your specific butt.

Maybe some people think BMW can make a nice seat. Maybe it's that guy who is 145 pounds of fit muscle and Roman gladiator ass. But you go to a BMW rally, and you see that about 90% of the bikes have a variety of replaced saddles, from Russells, Corbins, Sargeants, to Mayers. Apparently, this cottage industry saw how desperate we addicted fools were and decided to create the most euphoric icing on the cake to our disease of riding forever into the sunset—saddles that are so custom you feel like your ass is being fitted for a personally-tailored Armani.

"Oh, what color sir? You want a red strip, no yellow? Oh, you want the faux Ferrari leather pattern...oh, the real leather...yes, that will be an extra $200." Then they sit you on your bike and take pictures like you are a pin-up. The motorcycle seat maker shows up to all major motorcycle events and has a huge display. The $60,000 rig they pull up in to make seats on the spot shows how profitable this business is. And worth every penny.

Rocky, of Bill Mayers Saddles, tells me I need my seat an inch higher. He has me move all around the bike, slipping my crotch up to the tank, moving back like I would on long days to stretch. He analyzes me on my bike and keeps me there for a while until he says, "Ok, get off now." And they take it very seriously. Then his assistant rips my BMW saddle to the bare plastic backbone and starts building a work of art. He uses all kinds of different foam and spends hours carving it like a sculptor working on a medieval marble saint. This looks like science and art melding together. After many hours, he puts the white ivory foam seat back on my bike and tells me to go for a ride. He asks me to take notice of any discomfort, any hotspots or rubbing, any pain. He knows there won't be any. He even carved out space for the "boys."

I go ride for twenty minutes, taking note of any hotspots where my body makes contact with the surface of the foam seat. I explain in dizzying detail, getting all fussy about where the inside of my thighs had a slight burning sensation. Yes! This is motorcycling in 2014. The technician goes back to carving those areas on the foam where I felt pressure. Then another test ride until all is OK. Finally, my own custom upholstery job. That will be $350 please.

Once on the highway, I know it takes about 400 miles to break in the new saddle. The saddle has the shape of an old tractor seat covered with leather. On my 400-mile ride, I decide to go another 100 miles, then another 200 miles, and before I know it, I just spent 10 hours riding. No pain. What? Wow! Worth every dollar. Now my rides give me smiles instead of mental gymnastics to manage the pain. Best money spent. Hands down. So whether you ride a Beemer, Indian, or Honda, if your butt hurts, spend the cash. Ride and Enjoy! Enjoy is the operative word.

Some day the manufacturers, ahem BMW, will take note and hopefully take the time to engineer a proper saddle. But I am not waiting. "Hello, Rocky, I just bought another bike...."

MOTORCYCLE MEANDERINGS

THE TRIBE

I just read of a Wynonna Judd who was riding with her husband in South Dakota. She was on her own bike and ahead of him. He, for some unknown reason, swerved into oncoming traffic and is now fighting for his life in some unknown emergency room. For some reason I feel connected and concerned. I said a prayer.

Every time I hear of some biker who got hurt, I feel a twinge in my heart. How do I feel such connection with a total stranger? They don't know me, and I will never know them. Somehow their misfortune triggers an empathic note in my psyche. I wonder if our rare breed of experience creates some mythological connection like family, tribe, community in our collective conscious. Am I alone in the experience? I ride. They ride. We ride. We understand a common soulful experience. We take a risk with our lives to experience that spirit. I begin to slowly understand how other tribes, religions and cultures feel connected on a collective level. Who's to say this is not on a profoundly deep level, because it feels deep? Carl Jung might even validate us bikers for being so connected collectively.

Either way, I do my part. I send my concern, love, energy, prayers—whatever you want to call it—to that stranger in South Dakota fighting for his life, and for his wife supporting him by his side. Our tribe is universal. He is my brother, she is my sister. Our blood loves the same rumble of motor beneath us, the movement of our bodies in motion. Our soul connects to mother earth through two wheels on asphalt or dirt. We smell the air, feel the cold, get achy fingers, sweat in our leathers, sunburn our noses and get chapped lips. We live to be with our loved ones and friends on our bikes.

And when tragedy strikes one of us, we are struck too. We go deep into our humanity and find compassion for each other in this tough, old world that judges us for loving our dangerous lifestyle. Yes, what we do is dangerous. But no more dangerous than living fully alive. We carry the secret and sometimes hopelessly give up explaining it to those who are blind and do not see our people. Our tribe is not for all. It is Our Tribe.

TODAY'S BIKER, YESTERYEAR'S COWBOY

As I pull up to Reye's tavern off Highway 33 in a small town of twenty cabins, I feel like the old west is still very much alive. There is a bar that serves the only food in town, more like a village really. Watching bikers pull in to camp for the weekend, I think that if this were a hundred years ago, those would be horses, not Harleys, and those would be cowboy hats, not helmets, but the beer probably is the same. The bartender, Tony, is congenial as you could imagine a tavern owner to be. He knows my face and makes me feel welcome. Tomorrow is his 43rd birthday, and he is inviting everyone for free food. All his kids (there are a lot) are raised right here, playing with snakes and motorbikes in the countryside. I think things haven't changed that much for snakes and kids in the last hundred years. Except that the small motorbike is the new pony.

A cowboy was a self-reliant vagabond and believed that fresh air and real weather was a more inspiring way to find life than working in a courtroom or shipyard. It was a choice. They carried all the clothes on their ride for anything the weather could throw at them, be it 100-degree scorchers or sleet and snow. Most cowboys today are still basically self-employed entrepreneurs who move around like gypsies from ranch job to ranch job. We associate so much of the cowboy with their inseparable relationship to their horse. What would a cowboy be without a horse? What would a motorcycle rider be without a motorcycle?

So much of American identity is tied up with the myth of the cowboy. I wonder if the myth is real and still alive, but now with the present motorcycler on his iron horse. Our land invites us to explore. The USA is huge, and we are born into this collective consciousness of wide openness and the freedom to go wherever we can buy some gas. This is true for teenagers going camping in their Vanagans, retirees in their motorhomes, and motorcyclists crisscrossing the map on two wheels. We want to see Our country, experience Our land. Be free in it.

I think bikers, especially the ones that have been truly committed to the lifestyle for years, seem very unique. Is this the type of person who would have chosen the life of a true cowboy, owning only the horse and blanket back in 1870? Is there something American and primitive driving these people to buck the system? Has the land and mythology still carved some of us out for this lifestyle? Why do bikers seek out blue collar dives to feel at home? Why do we yearn for lonely deserts and mountain roads meandering with rushing rivers? Places where we can practice that Old West cowboy art of self-sufficiency. Is changing a tire on my dirt bike that different from changing a horseshoe?

As a biker, I find peak experiences that border spiritual mysticism by being out in God's country, in nature, on my metal horse. Life doesn't get more crystalline. I have space for peace and clarity. As I gaze at desert flowers or smell the mountain pines, I contemplate like a mystic, like an ascetic. Is this not what we associate with the American cowboy myth? That he is a man who knows things, who talks with spirits, who prefers his own company over false pretense, who shoots straight and honest, who speaks only enough. Did time in the saddle temper his immaturity and give him a calm that life in the droves could not? Did time amongst a natural world so much larger than him give him wisdom, gratitude, gentleness, and clean eyes that see men's souls?

We fear and respect the cowboy. Perhaps the seasoned motorcyclist really does continue their legacy. I believe in the myth of cowboys, in earnest. I do. I am.

MOTORCYCLE MEANDERINGS

GOODBYE MY FRIEND

Tonight I said goodbye to Pepe. I swore I would never let my dear friend go. They say never sell your true first motorcycle, the true first love. I did it. Tonight. I sat on him in the early darkness of night with a beer and reflected on memories. How can this steel frame and aluminum swing arm hold me and my soul? I don't know, but he does.

We became friends on the slopes of Southwest Colorado. I dropped him on the dirt a lot and even in a river, bending and scraping his metal appendages, and he kept plugging along. His scars—hundreds of them—are all memories of days I lived fully. Why did I let him go? Is it because he taught me real joy as my engagement to my fiancée was slowly dying? Did he give me new, life-giving blood while my job was draining all the life out of me? Did he hold my angst and pain and defeat, and now that I have healed I needed to let all that go?

I don't really know.

All I do know is that after I took him for one last rear wheel-sliding spin, I was ready to let go. I watched him go away in the back of someone's truck. Something I never thought I would do.

Last week I let go of my favorite ever sport tour BMW R1100S to buy the only cage I would ever miss owning, my Mazda Miata (closest a car can get to a motorcycle). In one week, I have let go of the two dream bikes I lusted over and worked and waited for, saving my pennies in anticipation, until

I lived my dream. I road those two bikes with my heart and smile every time.

Why am I gutting my garage of the things I love? On a dark, lonely Friday, no less? Leaving the supermarket tonight in my car to go sit and watch action movies with bachelor food, a gentleman on a custom rat cafe scrambler stopped his blatting bike to let me pass in front of him. He insisted. I hesitated and went forward. And I knew in that moment why I'm letting go of these lovely bikes I cherished. I have known it for months. I am going to build my own dream bike like this bloke. I will create my own dream bike from my truest playful vision.

As I head out of the parking lot, I get a picture text from the new owner of Pepe on my Iphone. My first real bike, in a stranger's garage. I text the new owner a promise to keep in touch and tell him all the stories of Pepe over beers in a Santa Barbara bar someday. Which I doubt will ever happen.

Too much.

DON'T TELL ME THE ODDS

When Han Solo yells at C3PO, "Never tell me the odds!" while entering an asteroid field in The Empire Strikes Back, I relate. There are some people out there that fret like the Star Wars robot. God Bless Them. They are annoying. I don't like telling anyone anymore that I ride motorbikes, for fear that they will spew off a diatribe of safety bullshit, warning me about how dangerous it is. Like I don't already know. "Hi, I ride a motorbike and therefore I must be a dumbass, who doesn't possibly know what is at stake."

Ironically I ride partly because I do know what is at stake and know its incredible value. Not only do these well-intending people tell me some horror story about someone they knew six degrees to Kevin Bacon that died or got maimed while riding, they must also look at me like I'm ignorant and judge my passion as pathological, a "phase" I will grow out of, like a pubescent teen trying out face piercings. It must be a "mid-life crisis" or an addiction. The warning is born of care and love, but reeks of condescension and self-righteousness. When we part ways, I can almost hear them praying that I find my way to the lord and learn how much of a sinner I was for possibly ever getting on that throbbing, evil, maligned, fire-breathing, gas-eating, two-wheeled beast that was prophesied in the book of Revelation.

So many times, the fact that I ride a bike comes out like a shameful confession, head down, which then elicits some graphic description of an accident they read about this week in the paper. What about the forty car fatalities that week? Nope, they find the one about the biker who was hit by a drunk driver three years ago at the corner of X and Y. I should hold my head higher and see if that works.

So I choose to talk about bikes with only those who bike. We get each other. I guess that's why Christians may prefer talking to Christians, or hippies with other hippies. There is a shared journey that is safe to explore without being damned, warned and shamed.

Why should someone be shamed for riding a motorcycle? That is silly. Silly I say. But those who drive cars? Now they are crazy.

IDIOT LIGHTS SUCK

If you drive a cage that is any newer than 1990, then you probably live with the infernal engine light. This light is in the silhouette of an engine and is usually glowing a disconcerting orange or red. "Danger Will Robinson!" Stupid light. Actually back in the day it was called an Idiot Light. And this Light does not even tell you what is wrong. At least the old dial on the dash signified some information—engine has low oil pressure or is too F'n hot. Now a computer runs your car and keeps you forever in mystery. You have to take your car to the dealer where they will "plug it in" and get some "codes" to tell the "mechanic" what's wrong. Even the mechanic is asked to not use his brain too much.

This Idiot Light incites fear, followed by that sinking feeling of wishing you had done the responsible car owner thing, like check your fluids more often. But nine times out of ten, the problem is something you probably would not have been able to solve on your own anyway. Chances are the problem is a blown sensor, which is electronic. So let me get this straight, my buddy just spent $700 on replacing sensors on his $3000 Jeep, just so the computer can work?! There was actually nothing wrong with the car and its functioning. Am I crazy, or is this just plain abuse of our human ingenuity? I want ingenuity back where it belongs—man and motor, not man and CPU.

Okay, enough energy spent talking about cages with four wheels. I bring all this up to show why motorcycles are still a saner mode of transport, and I also want to voice a clarion call to why we two-wheelers are in trouble if our bikes go the way of cars. I am deeply concerned about the encroaching computer messing with our steeds.

The new bikes are all starting to show up with brains. Electrical brains that process braking, acceleration, wheel slippage—pretty cool ideas, but there is a price. Sure you don't have to worry about whether you entered the turn too fast because an electronic traction control will think for the uninitiated. I, too, am tempted to buy a brand new bike because maybe I will be making stupid decisions that could cost me my life or leg. And yet, there is a price for giving up the freedom to learn the machine with blood and sweat and nerves. Do I really want a bike that can compensate? Won't I be tempted to be more stupid? Do I want technology to always replace skill, hard won and earned? By giving up my responsibility to learn carefully and practice judiciousness, am I not sacrificing real autonomy? I don't like all the questions these idiot lights make me think about.

As with cars, motorcycles are becoming so complex that many of us may be afraid to change the oil, brakes pads, or even lube our own chain. I can honestly say I have committed all three of these sins and am full of insecurity and a bit shameful that I have abdicated such a basic responsibility to my mechanic. But looking at how much I have spent on maintenance for my three bikes and not being able to honestly look myself in the mirror lately, I am of the conviction that I want to own bikes that don't intimidate me, that don't have Idiot Lights for this idiot. I want to hold the reigns again and learn to change my oil, drain and refresh my radiator, change spark plugs, maybe even change and balance a tire. I am better than just a motorcycle cleaner with soap and polishing wax.

If you are lucky enough, your motorcycle just has an oil or temperature light or gauge. Cheers to analog, and down with digital. It is consoling to the visceral mind to see a needle show you how much gas you have, how low your oil pressure is, how hot your motor is running. You can use the one or two sensors that are mechanical, not a computer chip, to tell you what is going on. If you are really lucky, your bike is still air-cooled, and you don't even need to worry about radiators, oil coolers, etc. Plain old, ancient million-year-old air keeps everything just fine. You need only to make sure there is some gas and oil. Just writing this makes me want to ditch my more modern bikes for an old mid-seventies Beemer, Indian, Guzzi, or Honda. Something simple.

Even if I get split nails, bloody knuckles, and smelly, greasy clothes, I sense I would be a more proud human. I want to understand the beast that carries me to new lands. It's a matter of relationship and self-respect.

But mainly, I am tired of being an ignoramus who is scared of idiot lights. Give me a wrench.

MOTORCYCLE MEANDERINGS

SKIING TAUGHT ME HOW TO RIDE, AND THAT LEADS TO LOVE

I grew up in the shadow of the Wasatch Mountains in Utah. I could stretch the truth and say that I learned to ski before I learned to walk, but my dad did have me on the wooden planks by 1st grade. I fell in love with skiing. It was a love affair that took years and years of rhythmically dancing to and fro in the snow, each day learning something new about my lover.

By the time I hit my teens I was officially a ski bum. I lived to let go and fly down the slope, back and forth thousands of times in one day. I thought that nothing could feel so good in body and soul. "Skiing is a dance, and the mountain always leads," reads a University of Alta t-shirt. I grew up skiing Alta and lived by this credo.

By the time I was thirty, I was driving through the Southwest with my dad, skiing all the resorts in the area. Little did I know I would live in Durango, Colorado someday and have an affair with motorbikes, leaving behind my first love of skiing. Not far from Durango, my dad and I found the longest ski run I had ever skied, at Telluride, "to-hell-u-ride." Wow, I could ski for twenty minutes straight and not even be done with the ride. To fly down the fall line and surrender to gravity, to feel the response of my input with the subtle movements of my twitchy muscles, to connect with the planet through my own speed was the ultimate Zen experience. I felt alive. I felt normal. The world finally made sense. All thinking stopped, and the artistic spirit met my soul. Bliss. Ecstasy. The stuff of Catholic mythology and union with God. I never tried to explain because I did not want to be shamed as a heretic.

This is how I would know the world until motorcycling at age 38. I don't ski anymore. I don't even miss it much. No more waiting in ski lift lines for ten minutes of skiing pleasure. For fifteen dollars of gas (versus a $100 ski pass), I can ride and carve the mountains for hours. The dance never has to stop until it is time to rest. And now not only can I dance mountains and canyons, but also deserts, salt flats, beaches, dunes, and all that nature can offer my spirit.

One time my old ex-fiancée rode on the back of my motorbike. She said, you ride like you ski. Yes, I do. I dance! It is romantic. I ride as I am in love. I ride like the wind. I pull up my visor and stick my nose into the brisk wind and fly. As I enter the first of hundreds of turns, I let the momentous rhythm take me like an entranced lover. I listen to the music of my motor and let my body listen by brail, melting into the seat of this vessel that delivers me to nature. I feel the rumble of its heart. There is a partnering, a collaboration. This is not just me anymore. I have a relationship to tend to. I partner with the machine, where man's ingenuity encounters Mother Nature; where rubber tire with motor meets dirt and asphalt.

As I swoop from one turn to the next there is a symphony, a dance of rising and falling, heaving and leaning into the sensuous contours of the mountain. To follow a stream, a river, a canyon bottom, a ridge of her mountain saddles, the skis taught me and led me to what every motorcyclist and good theologian or philosopher knows—freedom and love necessarily coexist.

TAKE THIS JOB AND SHOVE IT

Some of my warmest memories are driving down a dirt road with my brothers and dad at 5:00 in the morning to go hunt deer or ducks. Inevitably one of the three eight tracks we had was either Waylon, Willie, or Johnny Paycheck. As I soaked up "being" a man and felt the warmth of kin, I absorbed the outlaw country deep into my soul. The whole experience became one. The pinnacle moment as we drove through snow and mountains was listening to Johnny Paycheck sing, "Take This Job and Shove It...I aint working here no more." As I look back at my life, that song imprinted on me in dangerous ways.

One could look at my employment history and honestly say I lived that song. It became the gateway for courage to shun the shackles of bosses and onerous spirit-killing slave work.

Are you the professional that can't sleep at night? Is your head heavy with massive concerns about massive things that seem massively important? The recession, your equity, payments up to your neck, clients that think you should live and die for their plight. Maybe you are the auto mechanic, or the surgeon, or the attorney working with the downtrodden, or an all-too-serious pastor, high school administrator, social worker, welder, lawn mower. Does it really matter?

When I was an altar boy, the Ash Wednesday service always reminded me that we are ultimately dirt. Ashes to ashes, dust to dust. Well hell then, let me go ride some dirt and dust.

Let me tread with two wheels upon some soul who lived a thousand years ago, whose bones are dried and crushed to sand.

One day I will be the sand and dirt, giving nutrients to plants and getting caught in someone's greasy chain and sprocket. At least my journey will continue as vicarious witness to yet another rider's bliss.

It is two in the morning, after love making, and I can't get it out of my head that so many of us are up half the night thinking about how our work is so important. But we are dying for relief, for the weekend, for retirement, for freedom. What have we done believing that missiles are more important than riding in the wind, that Wall Street and their point system really can affect our moods, that our complaining clients are benefiting from our attention, that our taxes are so bloody important to pay or dodge?

When I was a kid, all that mattered was how lost I could get on my bike, or what kind of tobacco I could find to smoke behind a bush, or what girl I could play doctor with. Ok, I followed the bible and put away my childish ways. I became a man, only to discover I want to be free like a child again. Adult logic hardly makes sense. I get the idea of growing up, but that should not mean at the expense of joy.

We mostly work at jobs so to buy stuff in life. That is why up to 80% of all people stay at jobs that they hate. Apparently most heart attacks happen Monday mornings. No mystery there. Even a child can see the writing on the wall. Can you see the riding on the wall?

When the recession hit, our President said go spend some more. Well, if that is how it is going to be to save our economy, then let me spend my remaining credit on new tires, a new helmet, new leather, or a new exhaust that might add a few horsepowers for a thousand dollars. Better yet, let me buy 5 sets of tires to use this year. That's right, how about spend my last $6,000 on a two-week trip through the Swiss Alps on a BMW or Harley, or better yet Patagonia on a dual sport. That's right. Take this Job and Shove IT! I am going riding to play.

When my mother was in her early seventies she said, "I still feel like I am eighteen." Amen. When I was an eighteen-year-old high school senior, I visited her at her job. As I walked the maze of cubicles and saw old men who looked like broken-spirited drones, I got nauseous. Sick. A deep, spiritual unease and dread came over me. While in the cafeteria, I saw slumped men with noose ties around their necks. I uttered desperate words to my mother. I said, "If this is what growing up means, I don't think I can do this." My heart was dashed for I thought adulthood meant freedom to be my full self. My mother said in a very emphatic way, "You don't have to live this way." She encouraged me to follow my bliss and actually still does to this day. Thank God for mothers, and riding down dirt roads with Johnny Paycheck and kin.

MOTORCYCLE MEANDERINGS

SPEED ON THE S CURVES LIFTS MY SOUL

It is a gray day. Actually it's sunny, but it feels gray. I don't do well with the darkness of late fall turning into winter. Not enough day. Feeling more vampire, so I have managed to play hooky all week—blessing and curse of the self-employed. No whip to be cracked on my back, but I will pay the price next week. Actually, I'm already paying the price for my sloth. I'm selling one of my favorite bikes, so I can buy a "cage" for the dark, rainy drives of winter. This is a hard lesson I keep learning. I sell my seasonal car so I can just ride from spring through late fall. This affords me more money to buy more tires and more bikes for more rides. Such a glutton.

So now I need to sell my beloved BMW R1100S for $4500. I paid $6k this spring and rode the shit out of it. In six months, I doubled the mileage it took the first owner to make in thirteen years. I am a proud, haughty man, waiting for God to strike me, but I think he is kind of glad too that the Beemer was ridden hard and put away, hot and wet.

As I glumly search the want ads looking for a car and feeling so uninspired, I have an idea—what better way to distract myself than by going to look at motorcycles? Best way to grieve the loss of a bike is to get another one.

So I head over to my fellow motohead-brother's, dad's house. John and his dad have a love affair with motorcycles. John's dad has seven Honda motorcycles and a Yamaha to add icing on the cake. John and I are chiding and goading his dad to let go of the CX500 to us for a song of $1000, so we can make us a cafe racer. After some lunch at Taco Hell, I realize we really might be able to get that bike, and all of the sudden winter in Southern California does not seem so depressing. I know, I am soft, but having lived in Alaska for six years, my serotonin levels run for their lives at the sight of winter. My mind goes to wrenching in a warm garage, dreaming and creating a new beast.

So as I get on my trusty R1100S to take the long way home, I at least have some sense of hope and vision for this potential creation I might be riding in a few months. I take the country and canyon roads home, as I am learning to despise the drone of caged drones on the highway. I realize that I am also selling my bike because I have had dreams of crashing that bike, and several of my scary-accurate, intuitive friends called to ask if I had gotten into an accident. My own intuition says I need to get off the roads where cars act like mad ants. I need to leave my dear red dragon of a bike Beemer in someone else's hands, who will ride it where it excels, on the highways and autobahns of cars.

Today, as I rip up the canyons, I notice my spritely pace and realize that I love how damn fast this bike is. Turning the S's and S's and S's, slithering, snaking, I speed and know this winter will not separate me from my soul, like it has done so many times. My hope will not be taken away with my bike next week. My Beemer is a casualty of this fall, but I will build a new bike. And go fast.

TWO MOTORCYCLES STUCK TOGETHER

I had to buy a cage. Don't ask. Let's just say I was being a bit stupid, thinking I could live alone with three motorcycles and will definitely try that lifestyle as soon as possible again. I bought a convertible sports car as it seemed the closest thing to a motorcycle and the furthest from a 2-ton boring SUV. What "redeemed" my cage purchase and gave me hope was an experience the other day. I was driving like a mad devil up Highway 33 out of my Ojai home. It is like having Tail of the Dragon in your back yard for seventy miles one way, then seventy back. I live here because 33 exists, and I ride like I breathe—regularly.

After I whipped up fifteen miles of curvy tarmac, cranking "Thunderstruck" and "Money Talks" by AC/DC, I parked the top-down sports car at the top to see the view. Kept the music blaring in the dirt parking lot and admired the mountains, ocean and islands off Ventura, Californ-I-A. Then two rogue, old riders pulled up on motorcycles. A cruiser and sport tourer, they were an odd couple and a true sign that all bikers are brothers. Old guys lose the ego and realize that all two-wheelers are in the same game together. I decided to turn off AC/DC to be brotherly.

A kind gent was sophisticated enough to say in the first words of his helmet coming off, "That car you have is just two motorcycles stuck together." Out of the mouths of wise men! I needed that. I was feeling like I had let my soul down by getting a car. I had anguished for six months, researching every known car that could give me joy like a motorcycle. I realized I could not.

But if I have to drive a cage every now and then, at least let it be the spirit of the bike in the form of a sports car with heart. Come to think of it, I had driven that car like a bat out of hell to feel the G-force on my body. It was a poor man's attempt at feeling a tenth of the sensation I experience on the wealth of a motobike.

But that man's words honored my agony. He recognized that my Mazda Miata was my attempt at saving my soul and holding on to my dignity. Two motorcycles put together. Seeing how I drive it, I better get that racing roll cage. Next song, Highway to Hell.

SAFETY

I think if one is to live long while riding motorcycles, they eventually need to deal with the fundamental question, "Am I going to ride with my lizard brain that is millions of years in development, or am I going to use the newest technology evolution has given me, the bigger brain made of fat cells, ie. my frontal lobes?" Am I going ride like a dumb ape or a smart one? Some apes ride harder and die harder, and I am full believer that it is one's god-given right to do so. But as Reg Pridmore, former world motorcycle racing champion and owner of a riding and racing school says, "Good riders are thinking riders." He argues effectively that the fastest and best racers are those that use their intelligence and think their way to victory.

I, like the next rider, love riding from my sphincter and sex organs. That primal scream at the throttle is fuckin amazing. That's why I ride. But in order for me to keep doing what I love, I am beginning to think I need to use all of my brain. I have been told (and I know) that I am thinking man. Sometimes I wish I could turn off that part of me, as I sure do enjoy life more without over-thinking. Truly, the happiest souls are those that just live and don't overanalyze everything. Go red in your neck, and the sun will burn away all the neurotic from the bottom of your brain stem. But I need to move beyond my concrete simplicity and start to also account for dangers beyond my periphery. I need to expand my horizons in all facets, not just the road.

When it comes to staying alive on the road, it is time to put that neurotic analyzer to work. That's part of why I ride, so I can engage 100% of my brain, so I can Zen out, be present in my life, philosophize, be creative and feel alive. My ADHD mind finally isn't bored and is fully entertained with computing the variables of all the data my mind is taking in at 90mph, rolling through a turn. I size up asphalt texture, oil spots for freshness, sand or debris in my way, shrubs sticking out to grab me, sun in my view or shade-hidden textures ahead, squirrels darting back and forth, deciding whether they want to die today. Assessing wind, rain and heat, the sound of my motor, the speed and adhesion of rubber on asphalt, the oncoming truck I can sense is too close to the yellow line with their side mirrors ready to fracture my shoulder. God! It is engaging fully. All of these diagnostics are given a mere millisecond of instantaneous recognition while I contemplate my mortality and what my soul is to do in this world.

I may be an ape, but I also know when to just ease off the throttle, a smart ape. So for now it is Ride for the Slide, check the bike pre-flight like a pilot, sign up for more dirt and road classes and track days, buy new gear, read more bike porn (for the articles!), dive more into my passion with whole heart, and use as much of my brain as possible.

It's simple for this simple mind. I don't want to miss tomorrow's ride.

AUTUMN IS HERE

Today I was the only motorcyclist on the road in little old Ojai, California. It's autumn now, and we soft Californians are running for hot soup because the first rains are here. The chill in the air has turned the daily high of 85 last week to something like 71 today, and a few drops of spatter fall on the road, making rainbow puddles emerge from the asphalt. I play with the oil spots and ride around them like an obstacle course game.

Autumn used to be my favorite season, and biking has changed all that. I want perpetual spring. I don't own a car this time of year. I sold my old Beemer 328i four months ago, and its seems I just can't get around to buying another cage. But sure enough, when the winter rains hit I will finally buy one.

Autumn seems to bring some morose feelings today. Even though I usually love riding in weather, California has spoiled me with the last seven or eight months of perfect weather. I know, I am entitled. Spoiled is the word. When I read about guys in Alaska who put their steeds away for six months, the realization hits that I expect to ride every day, whenever I want.

The closing of daylight also hinders the prospects of really long days and adventures. So what will I do this winter? If I was still an addictive skier, winter would be my season, but now I am ruined because I live for dry pavement wherever it can be found. And I'm not much of a wrencher who spends all winter tinkering with bikes, although I wish I were. Track days, if I can pull enough cash together, sound fantastic. Maybe it's time to do one track day per month and a safety course. Or better yet, a dirt bike class to build real skills instead of winging it.

What I really need to do is go chase spring and summer. Now that sounds like a good life. Yep, it's time to follow through on my twenty-years dream of going to Patagonia. What could be more enticing than riding to Torres del Paine? Hmm, now do I fly into Chile or Argentina? Rent? Buy? Winter is actually starting to seem bearable....

The sound of raindrops interrupts this winter dream. It's going to rain today, again. Now where did I put those new waterproof insulated gloves?

BONNEVILLE SALT FLATS WITH POPS

My pops and I used to wake at the darkest hour right before dawn, to go hunting, fishing, boating or skiing. Today, I met him down in his living room in the wee hours. Of course he was already showered, coffee-ed, and reading the paper...waiting. We have our regular routine of doing what needs done and slipping out the door without waking my mother. My dad is 81-years-old and actually asked, "Are we taking your motorcycle or the car?" Right then I wish I owned a Gold Wing or Harley bagger with armrests so my old man could sit in style. Paradoxically, we opted for dad's Lincoln Towncar instead and drove two hours to Wendover, Utah, making our usual pit stop for McDonald's coffee.

Most Salt Lakers (Lickers) have not been to the world famous Bonneville Salt Flats. This is the place of heroes. This is the Vatican of speed freaks. And this particular week was for vintage bikes to test their metal.

One of those most encouraging things I witnessed out there on the flat white stuff was seeing the people. I will get to the bikes in a minute. For some primal reason, I have always watched the world, looking for heroes to show the way, prophets to light my path. When I was a ski bum, I noticed older guys still tearing it up. When I was a surfer, I would go hang out in god's bathtub with the fifty, sixty, and seventy-year-olds to watch the sunrise before work. These men, these Zeus-like figures, were and still are living the dream. And they live on the Bonneville Salt Flats as well.

They are my role models like my dad. My pops is eighty-one and still skiing. So here we are at Bonneville, and that movie with Anthony Hopkins playing Burt Munro in The World's Fastest Indian, is very accurate to what I am seeing. Most men out at the BUB Motorcycle Speed Trials are well into the white salt-and-pepper stage, reaching for the blue horizon. They have that glint in their eyes, much like I would imagine Burt Munro. These are living mythological beings who are trying their damnedest to fly on two wheels.

And it warms my hackles to see so many women out there as well, but that is for another essay. I will just say whoever has the benefit of knowing, dating, and marrying one of these women is so damn lucky.

I found myself having hope. I could see myself someday out there with a bike that speaks to the little boy inside who yearns to go fast, very fast. What is it about speed that feels so good to my body and psyche? I don't want to explore that inner question much for fear that I will ruin it with my western analytical mind. Like sex, good whiskey and dark chocolate, I want that desire to go unchallenged.

Back to the old guys. So this one guy is out there with his fifth wheel and wife. She takes all the time in the world to talk passionately about how he holds the record with a diesel KLR. Turns out he is the first guy to supply motorbikes to the military since the WWII Harleys and Indians. I am never surprised to find entrepreneurial heroes out here, as there must be something about entrepreneurial risk-taking and motorcycles. These old guys are not your run of the mill hamster wheel types. They were built to think outside the cubicle box of our culture. They put diesel motors in dirt bikes and sell them to the marines. Then they sell the company and bring their sweetheart out to the blinding hot salt flats, so she can speak with loving pride of her man, who just made a diesel Enduro bike and put it into a cafe configuration, then tucked it into a streamlined art deco metal shell, turbo-ed it and is leathering up and heading out to beat some elusive mph mountain that needs to be climbed.

For every person I greet and meet, there is some grand story of a full life living to the edge, the horizon. These are modern Mercury men and women with wings on their wheels made from the salt of the earth. Men like my father, who paved his own way in life and kept the joy despite the highs and lows. It seems they knew the secret that life was ethereal and brief, so they made some good choices.

Everyone appears to have a smile. No worries, except 'will my bike go faster?' Sounds childlike. It is natural, even logical. The salt has melted time and anxiety like it does ice. The heat, the sun, are scorching us all, and we are blinded by white. Our skin is frying red like the screaming motors. We are joining our environment on our machines, truly becoming one in the vast ancient lakebed.

On the salt all is level, flat, eternal and fleeting.

MOTORCYCLE MEANDERINGS

WHAT MOTORBIKE SPEAKS TO YOUR SOUL?

This last year has been tough. My last two bikes just were not doing it for me. I felt stuck. I knew the bikes I had were fun and full of heart. But they lacked soul. I did not realize how important it was for a rider to truly resonate with their motorcycle. It is crucial.

So I sold the bikes. And waited. And waited. Finally, one reached out to me. The second I saw a photograph of it I was intrigued. I knew from past experience that this is how it all starts. The obsession, the research on the internet, the pining, the shopping, the hunt was on.

And finally, I found the one that would work. A low mileage, 6 year old bike, that had been garaged. Got it for a song.

And now, I am back. All is redeemed. Riding a bike that will soon be my new friend, going on adventures. My life is complete again, soul mates joined. Bikes are funny that way. They are alive.

Now as I ride out into the desert I have my meditation back. I have a life giving activity that allows me to find my rhythm with my own life. Perspective, humor, joy, contemplation, balance are back. Neurosis is checked once again. I only realize now that that eight months without a bike was harder than I thought.

In that eight month period I fell apart.

For some, art, yoga, surfing, skiing, or running provides sanity. For me, it is riding my motorcycle. And I don't see this ending. Until I end.

As I come to realize just how important riding is, I am making peace with who I am. Acceptance. I need soulful attachments in this short life. Whether it be good food, good drink, good friends, or good motorcycles. I don't have time anymore for things that don't seem right. That includes bikes that don't speak to me. Bikes are not tools like a lawnmower or a chain saw. They are soulful art. Or they should be anyway.

So I found the one that speaks to me. A Moto Guzzi Griso.

What speaks to you?

WANDER LUST

I often see the bumper sticker, "Not all who wander are lost." I would like my own sticker that says, "all who wander lust." I lust to wander. I will be the first to admit I commit this sin daily on my bike.

It's too bad theologians and priests have ruined the word lust. They have demonized a natural primal urge, like our sexuality, to create an internal conflict. Lust implies a lack of control that leads us down a dark path. Fuck...so be it then. America would have never been discovered without such lust.

I look at lusting for what is around the next corner as a curiosity for life's surprises. Many times I ride just because I want to go get lost and find something new. It has the same creative energy I feel when experiencing my partner. Let me get lost in my lover, in the unknown world. I won't ask permission, and I will gladly confess, for I don't consider this lust sinful at all. Rather I believe it is a god-given urge, better yet goddess-given. Eros and Aphrodite fused on two wheels.

How many times do I just get on my bike and go? It starts with a vague sense of wanting to see something new. This subtle impulse beckons me, like a lover's whisper, to follow the narrow thread of pavement to the curves in the road, the breast in the next hill or navel of the next valley. I want to get lost in her, in this world of unknown mystery. I want to ride into her.

Other times I have a very strong sense that I need to go on a planned journey, knowing that the only planned thing about it is the starting point. I will end up wandering countless roads and dirt highways that call me to go explore. I intuit in the moment and give myself permission to lust after some little teasing path that was not on the map. There is no judgment; there is only curiosity and instinct, allowing myself to follow the pheromone trail to the next gas station, restaurant or beer joint that looks the most alluring.

Sometimes I choose a random road because a stretch of ocean fog offers solace and Zen, or the air feels cooler on the country farm roads. Every road's temperament has her charm. Even the rain is like a strong woman with an honest tongue—challenging and refreshing, washing away the dry, caked-on desert dirt of real sins. Like the sin of living a hamster wheel, "civilized" existence where aggression is rewarded. Is not the wander luster a more peaceful human authentic savage than the "controlled" Victorian puritan who is safely saved from the sin of lust, yet sinning daily against his brother with passive aggressive invisible daggers? Because he is not free, truly free? The wander luster is judged by the machine, the priest, the industrial admonition to keep working, keep the cogs going. I am more interested in making sure the cogs of my sprocket are clean and lubed, ready for the next ravenous moment, not wasted on producing some widget that will take others further from their reality.

So go wander. Go lust. Get off the wheel, and get on your wheels. Get lost in the sanity and joy of surrendering to the open road. Trust your bike, trust yourself. Go, I say. Go.

WANDER LUST

ACKNOWLEDGMENTS

Editor: Amber Lennon
Cover: Kristen Smith
Formatting: Red Wheelbarrow Design

ABOUT THE AUTHOR

Johnny was raised to see the world. His mother gave him the longest of leashes as he explored the world 10 miles away at age 10 on his bike. He was allowed to climb on minibikes at an early age. Since then, he is embarrassed to tell people about his life because even when he tries people tend to not believe him, so he doesn't. He is more interesting in the present anyway. But to be brief: He has had eight lives and is working on number nine. Most of his life has been spent running rivers, skiing mountains, sailing, sea kayaking and surfing the oceans, trekking the remote mountain ranges in the world, hunting, fishing, and mostly hanging out around campfires. He finally 'settled down' when he accidentally rediscovered motorcycles in his late thirties. His restless soul is now at peace. He has found his true home on everything two wheels, which includes writing about it.